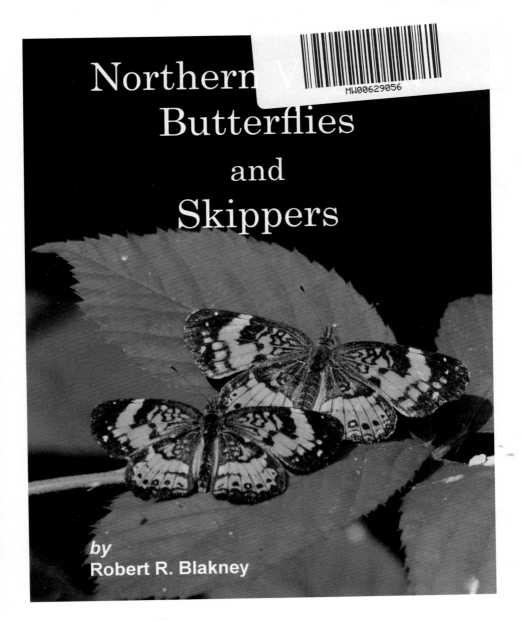

Northern V Butterflies and Skippers

by
Robert R. Blakney

ISBN-13:978-0692383490

Printed in the United States of America

Dedication This book is dedicated to Jim Waggener who has diligently led and inspired a group of citizen scientist volunteers in surveys of the Potomac River refuges, local parks and the Meadowood Special Recreation Management Area. The data compiled by Jim starting in the1990's contains invaluable information on the flora and fauna over the years and was referenced in the creation of this field guide.

Acknowledgments I would also like to thank the dedicated survey volunteers: Ana Arguelles, Bryan and Colleen Cloyed, Judy Kenyon, Su Kim, Ken Larsen, Jim Lingebach, Laura McDonald, Rusty Moran, Elena Meyer, Gary Myers, Matt Myers, Sheryl Pollock, Mike Ready, Dick Smythe, Bob Studholme, Jack Thorsen, Larry Underwood and Roger Verley. All are dedicated naturalists that provided inspiration for the pursuit of citizen science and good companionship on the surveys where most of the photos in this book were taken. Special thanks to Ana Arguelles, Rusty Moran, Mike Ready and my wife Betsy for their editing help - it was invaluable. Thanks also goes to those listed below for generously contributing photographs.

Photos used in this book were contributed by the author and:
Ken Larsen (KL):   Pages: 13, 14, 49, 50,52, 56, 61, 63, 64, 65.
Rusty Moran (RM):   Pages: 14, 31, 41.
Gary Myers (GM):   Pages: 18, 19, 22, 26, 27, 35, 39, 42, 46, 50, 51, 56, 61, 63, 64.
Sheryl Pollock (SP): Pages: 6, 11, 30, 50, 56.
Michael Ready (MR): Pages: 26, 43, 41, 64.

References
Books:
A Swift Guide to Butterflies of North America, Jeffrey Glassberg
Butterflies of the East Coast, Rick Cech and Guy Tudor
Butterflies of Indiana: A Field Guide, Jeffrey E. Belth
Butterflies of North America, Jim P. Brock and Kenn Kaufman
The Butterflies of North America, James A. Scott
Useful Web Sites:
Audubon Society of Northern Virginia http://www.audubonva.org
Friends of the Potomac River Refuges http://www.foprr.org
Loudoun Wildlife Conservancy   http://www.loudounwildlife.org
Lep Log   https://leplog.wordpress.com
North American Butterfly Association http://www.naba.org

Table of Contents

Purpose and Scope The purpose of this field guide is to assist someone who has a new interest in butterflies, with a manageable reference for learning how to identify the species likely to be encountered in the Northern Virginia area. This guide covers 90 species that with a bit of effort should be found most years. The species covered can be found within one or two hours drive from most locations in Northern Virginia and most were found and photographed in the following four sites: Occoquan National Wildlife Refuge, Julie J. Metz Memorial Wetland Preserve, Occoquan Regional Park and the Meadowood Special Recreation Management Area. Finding a few species may require a short trip to Loudoun County or Southern Maryland and the Shenandoah National Park.

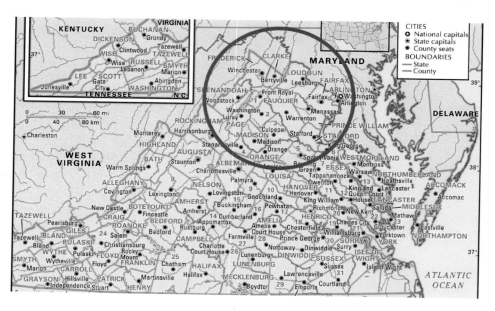

In Virginia there are several thousand moth species, about 98 butterfly species and about 58 skippers. The index lists all butterflies that have been found in the area within the last few years, and for those covered in this book, the page location.

Many butterflies are sexually dimorphic - females are visually different from males. In the species descriptions, where this is notable, the females are shown on the right and the males on the left.

Introduction Butterflies and skippers are 6-legged insects with 2 pairs of wings. The wings are scaled (scales are modified hairs) that are spread across the wings in overlapping rows. The scales refract light and produce many different colors. Other than their wings, butterflies have three main body parts: head, thorax and abdomen. On their head, butterflies have compound eyes, and a coiled proboscis used for feeding on nectar. On either side of the proboscis, butterflies have scaly mouth parts called palps that are used as feeding sensory organs.

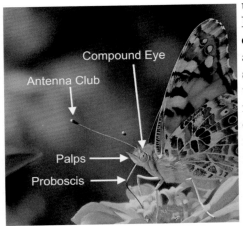

Butterflies also have two long clubbed antennae, which are additional sensory organs. The shape of the antennae is often used to differentiate butterflies from moths, as moths' antennae either lack a club or have a feathery tip (male moths). Most moths are not active during the day and if discovered will rapidly fly to cover. Butterflies on the other hand, are only active during the day and often only when there is sunlight. There are always exceptions to the general rules however, as there are species of nectaring moths that may occasionally be encountered. The diagram below shows the main terms used in this field guide.

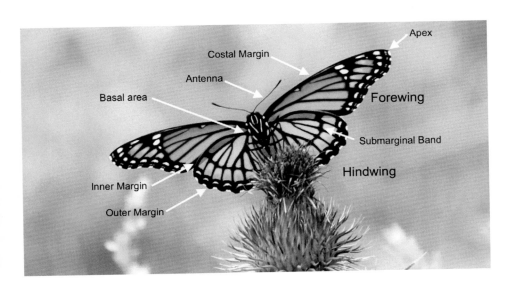

Life cycle of butterflies

Butterflies go through 4 stages: egg, larva (caterpillar), pupa (chrysalis) and adult butterfly – a complete metamorphosis. This process can take as little as a month or as long as a year depending upon the species. Some butterflies only reproduce once per year, others three to four times. Butterflies generally lay their eggs on a plant that is suitable for their caterpillar to eat. When the caterpillars hatch from their eggs, they eat and grow at a rapid rate molting and discarding their outgrown skin several times. When the caterpillar has grown sufficiently it will enter the pupal stage. Inside the chrysalis, the caterpillar changes into a butterfly, emerging from the chrysalis when conditions are right. Many butterflies overwinter in their chrysalis; others like the Mourning Cloak hibernate in leaves and still others like the Monarch fly south to hibernate in upland forests.

Most butterflies have at least two broods during the year – a spring and summer brood - but this can vary depending upon length of season and availability of suitable host plants. Each butterfly description in this guide will include the likely fly dates in our area and suggestions for where to find the more uncommon butterflies.

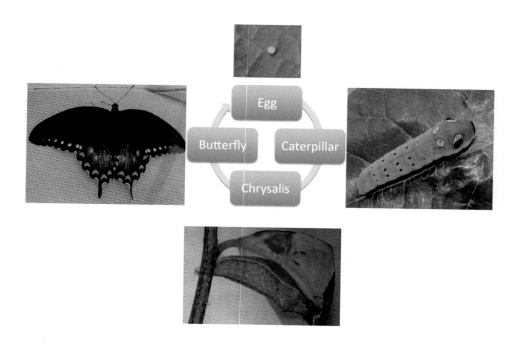

Butterfly caterpillars almost always require very specific host plants. If the host plant(s) are absent, the species will be locally absent unless the butterfly migrates from a distant area. Plants used by butterflies for nectar are not necessarily related to the plants needed by their caterpillars for food. Northern Virginia has a number of butterflies every year that probably do not breed in our area but migrate from the south. Some of the notable species that do this include Cloudless Sulphur, American Snout, and Ocola Skipper – all usually show up in early summer or early fall, sometimes in large numbers. Some have their first annual brood in the southern states and then move north for a second brood in our area before migrating south for the winter, like the Monarch butterfly. This is greatly dependent on plant cycles; when plants die back, butterflies have to wait until the next season or move on.

Butterfly taxonomy

Butterflies and skippers are insects in the order Lepidoptera. Taxonomists have divided Lepidoptera into a number of "superfamilies", all but two of which are moths. These two families are Papilionoidea (true butterflies) and Hesperioidea (skippers). Butterflies have been divided into six families:

Swallowtails *(Papilionoidae)* are our largest butterflies and all have hindwing tails. Six species may be found in this area. An interesting family, as most (except Giant and Zebra Swallowtail) mimic the Pipevine Swallowtail, which because its caterpillars eat the toxic pipevine plant gain a measure of protection from bird predators.

Whites and Sulphurs *(Pieridae)* are medium-sized butterflies that are mostly white or yellow. Eight species normally occur in the area.

Gossamer-wings *(Lycaenidae)* are predominantly blue, gray or brown butterflies. 16 species normally may be found in this area.

Metalmarks *(Riodinidae)* are not usually found in the area but may be found within an hour or so in southern Pennsylvania or western Maryland. This guide shows only the Northern Metalmark as an example.

Brushfoots (Nymphalidae) are quite diverse, of medium to large size, and among our most colorful butterflies that include fritillaries, crescents, checkerspots, anglewings, ladies, admirals, emperors, satyrs and the Monarch. Twenty-five or more brushfoots may be found in this area. They often appear to only have 4 legs as the shorter front pair are usually tucked behind the head.

Skippers *(Hesperiidae)* are about as closely related to butterflies as some moth superfamilies. They can be very difficult to identify in the field and have been divided into two subfamilies, Spread-winged Skippers *(Pyrginae)* and Grass Skippers *(Hesperiinae)*. We have 13 Spread-winged Skippers and about 20 Grass Skippers that can usually be found in the area. Unlike other butterflies, skippers have a relatively thick thorax. Grass skippers also differ in that when perched they tend to hold their forewings at a 45 degree angle to the ground, as do several of the Spread-winged skippers.

Note: the butterflies in this guide are not always shown in taxonomic order - confusing species are grouped together to more easily see the differences.

Identifying butterflies
Many of our butterflies are fairly easy to identify with a bit of practice, however a few notes of caution and things to look for.
- Is it a butterfly? As discussed earlier, moths fly mostly at night and butterflies during the day; butterflies have clubs at the end of their antennae and moths do not.
- Butterflies sometimes mimic one another. A good example of this is the dark colored Swallowtails. There are often subtle differences between the Pipevine Swallowtail (which is poisonous to birds) and the dark form of the Eastern Tiger Swallowtail, the Spicebush Swallowtail and the Black Swallowtail – they too would like to not be eaten.
- Skippers are hard – Grass Skippers even harder. Having a good pair of binoculars makes this problem a bit more manageable, however, making a photograph and sorting them out later is often the best solution – small super zoom cameras work well for this task.
- Some butterflies vary significantly between broods. This is caused by a number of factors such as the weather, season (how intense the sunlight is) and the plants available to the caterpillars. Some species can show significant size differences and color changes. For example, Sulphurs tend to show more intense colors in the Summer and less so in the Spring.
- Finally, as butterflies age, especially in the longer lived species, colors fade which can make identification difficult or impossible even for the expert.

Where to find butterflies Butterflies can be found almost anywhere, but they like flowers and sunshine. It is sometimes remarkable that when clouds cover the sun, butterflies seem to disappear – when the sun comes out again, butterflies are everywhere. Usually the temperature needs to be at least 60 degrees Fahrenheit for butterflies to be active. Certain butterflies like different habitats so if you are looking for a specific species, you need to head to the right place. The following are some suggestions that offer unique habitats and plants:
- Flower gardens offer nectar sources to butterflies and many species of butterfly are drawn to them – Swallowtails, White and Sulphurs and many of the Brushfooted butterflies.
- Roadsides and gravel roads offer different kinds of flowering plants that often draw butterflies to edge plants. The road surface often provides puddles and mineral deposits that some butterflies gain nutrients from.
- Old fields can be particularly good because they are a great place to find nectar sources such as thistles, milkweeds, mints, violets and clover – plants butterflies like a lot.
- Woodland trails are a good place to find Satyrs – they rarely stray beyond the forest edges. Forest edges are one of the best places to find Elfins and Hairstreaks. Most of them have a short season, so it is best to look during their predicted fly dates.
- Wetlands and bogs can be very rewarding because there are a few rare butterflies that you will not find anywhere else.

When searching for butterflies, knowing how will help greatly in finding them.
- Walk slowly so as not to startle them.
- Look for wet areas and nectar sources – don't overlook rotting fruit and dung.
- Look for host plants for the caterpillars - like milkweed.
- Look for the highest point – male butterflies often patrol high points looking for female butterflies.

Enjoy the adventure and I hope you find this guide useful.

Pipevine Swallowtail *Battus philenor*

Identification: Similar to Spicebush swallowtail, but note white spots on hindwing - they are more removed from the margin than on the Spicebush. Also there is only a single row of orange spots on the underside of the hindwing where the Spicebush has two.

Flights: (Uncommon) 3 broods from May to early October.

Host Plants: Pipevine - Aristolochia tomentosa.

This is an uncommon butterfly, probably because the host plant is uncommon. Look for the Pipevine plant and you are more likely to find the butterfly.

Spicebush Swallowtail *Papilio troilus*

Identification: Upperside: Iridescent blue-green clouding on hindwing, especially in males. White spots on forewing diverge. Underside: Two rows of orange spots and one blue-green spot.

Flights: (Common) Two overlapping broods from early April through September.

Host Plants: Spicebush, sassafras.

Zebra Swallowtail   *Eurytides marcellus*

Identification: Black and white zebra stripes. The sexes are similar.

Flights: (Common) Three flights from March through September. The first brood is usually more numerous. The second and third brood can usually be recognized by noticeably longer tails.

Host Plants: Pawpaw.

Black Swallowtail

Papilio polyxenes

Identification: Black with yellow spots on upperside. Note the parallel spots on the forewing that extend to the apex - this makes the swallowtail fairly recognizable in flight. The underside hindwing has two rows of orange spots.

Flights: (Common) Two or three flights from April through October.

Host Plants: Queen Anne's Lace and others of the carrot family.

Giant Swallowtail   *Papilio cresphontes*

Identification: Our largest North American butterfly and rare in the area, but every year some can be found. Easy to recognize by size and the yellow band that stretches from apex to apex.

Flights: (Rare) Two broods, May through August.

Host Plants: Hercules Club.

Eastern Tiger Swallowtail *Papilio glaucus*

Identification: The Eastern Tiger Swallowtail comes in two main colors - yellow and black. The black forms are always female. The yellow form is quick to distinguish from our other swallowtails, but the females usually require a closer look. The upper side hindwing usually shows a dark postmedian band and dark tiger stripes are usually visible in good light. Also, the underside hindwings have a single marginal orange spot band and the abdomen shows no spots like the Pipevine, Spicebush and Black Swallowtails.

Flights: (Abundant) Two to three overlapping broods, May through mid-October.

Host Plants: Tulip Tree and Black Cherry.

Checkered White   *Pontia protodice*

Identification: Similar to Cabbage White except multiple forewing spots: females are more heavily marked and have dark hindwing margins.
Flights: Rare and sporadic migrant, June through August, from south and west.
Host Plants: Shepperd's Purse, Virginia Peppergrass.

Cabbage White   *Pieris rapae*

Identification: Wings are white with a smoky apex and one black spot on the forewing on males and two on females. The underside is white or slightly yellow. This was originally a European butterfly.
Flights: (Abundant) From March through November.
Host Plants: Mustard family and cultivated cabbage.

Falcate Orangetip   *Anthocharis midea*

Identification: Small to medium butterfly with a hooked (or Falcate) forewing tip that is mostly white. Males have orange tips and both males and females have dark marbling on the underside surface.

Flights: (Common in season) One, between March to late May.

Host Plants: Various mustards - Hairy and Small-flowered Bittercress.

Orange Sulphur   *Colias eurytheme*

Identification: Orange Sulphurs are typically orange-yellow and the underside forewing is typically a darker yellow than the hindwing. Orange and Clouded Sulphurs are seasonally variable. Spring and fall broods are smaller and darker, and grayish-green scales obscure the yellow on the underside of the hindwings. This makes the Spring/Fall forms of the Orange and Clouded Sulphur difficult to separate. Both species have a white (or alba) form that are females. Orange and Clouded sulphurs do hybridize so field separation is not always possible.

Flights: (Abundant) Multiple overlapping broods from March through November.

Host Plants: Pea family, Clover, Alfalfa.

18

Clouded Sulphur   *Colias philodice*

Identification: Clouded Sulphurs tend to be a pale greenish-yellow and the underside wing base color typically shows little variation. See Orange sulphur discussion for variations.

Note: *The upper left photograph depicts a female Orange Sulphur flying with a male Clouded Sulphur - they often fly together.*

Flights: (Common) Multiple overlapping broods from April through November.

Host Plants: Clovers.

Cloudless Sulphur   *Phoebis sennae*

Identification: A large greenish-yellow sulphur on the underside with sparse orange-red spots. The spots on the females are more blotchy.
Flights: (Uncommon) Overlapping broods to the south of Virginia and butterflies show up on an irregular basis, May through October.
Host Plants: Partridge Pea and Wild Senna.

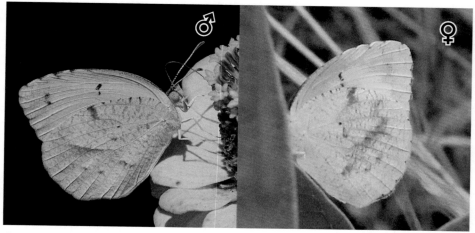

Sleepy Orange   *Eurema nicippe*

Identification: Male is bright golden-orange with rusty bands; the females are more yellow with more pronounced rusty bands.
Flights: (Uncommon) 2 broods, April to early November.
Host Plans: Sennas, Wild Sensitive Plant and Partridge Pea.

Little Yellow   *Eurema lisa*

Identification: Our smallest yellow that varies from orange to lime-yellow. The underside has scattered rusty spots. Note the two tiny black spots near the hindwing base - these are diagnostic.
Flights: (Rare) Overlapping broods to the south, irregular in Virginia
Host Plants: Sennas, Wild Sensitive Plant and Partridge Pea.

Dainty Sulphur   *Nathalis iole*

Identification: The smallest sulphur that is only slightly larger than our Gossamer-wing butterflies. Upper wings (not shown) have black tips and black bars on the leading edge of hindwing and trailing edge of forewing - I have not seen them land with open wings.
Flights: (Rare) Strays into our area on occasion in early fall.
Host Plans: Asters, particularly Spanish Needles.

21

Harvester   *Feniseca tarquinius*

Identification: A small orange and brown butterfly on top and orange spots circled with white below.
Flights: (Uncommon) Probably two broods between April and September.
Host Plants: Butterfly lays eggs next to Wooly Aphid colonies that live on Alder or Maple - caterpillars consume the aphids not plants.

American Copper   *Lycaena phlaeas*

Identification: Small orange and gray-brown butterfly. The dark forewing spots on males are typically less pronounced.
Flights: (Common) 3 broods from April through August.
Host Plans: Sheep Sorrel and Curly Dock.
Can be found in upland fields and road sides - Big Meadows at Shenandoah National Park is a good place to look.

Coral Hairstreak   *Satyrium titus*

Identification: Forewing brown with row of dark spots, Hindwing without tails and a row of orange spots and without blue patch. The sexes are similar.
Flights: (Uncommon) One brood in June.
Host Plants: Cherries and plums

Brown Elfin   *Deciduphagus augustinus*

Identification: Wings are red-brown and lack any accents and are not frosted.
Flights: (Uncommon) One brood in late April.
Host Plants: Huckleberry, Highbush & Lowbush Blueberry.

Striped Hairstreak — *Satyrium liparops*

Identification: Forewing with several offset white lines, hindwing blue patch capped with orange.
Flights: (Uncommon) One brood in late May to early July.
Host Plants: Cherries and plums.

Banded Hairstreak — *Satyrium calanus*

Identification: Forewing band bordered with white on one side. Blue patch same size or slightly larger than orange patch.
Flights: (Uncommon) One brood from June to early July.
Host Plants: Walnuts, oaks and hickories.

Frosted Elfin   *Callophrys irus*

Identification: Can be very similar to Henry's below but note the eye-spot and the short tail. Of all the Elfins, only the Frosted and Henry's have tails.
Flights: (Rare) One in late April to late May.
Host Plants: Yellow Wild Indigo.

Henry's Elfin   *Callophrys henrici*

Identification: Similar to Frosted but *without eye-spot*
Flights: (Common) One in early April to early May. Flies when the Redbud's are in bloom.
Host Plants: Redbud, American Holly and Winterberry.

Eastern Pine Elfin   *Callophrys niphon*

Identification: The wings have distinct white and brown lines on brown background.
Flights: (Uncommon) One extended brood from late March to mid-June.
Host Plants: Virginia and White Pine.

Juniper Hairstreak   *Callophrys gryneus*

Identification: Our only green butterfly. The underside is emerald green with white bands.
Flights: (Uncommon) Probably two overlapping from mid-April to mid-July.
Host Plants: Eastern Red Cedar

White M Hairstreak *Parrhasius m-album*

Identification: A large tan hairstreak with one white line. The line is shaped like a M or W on the hindwing near a red spot. Also note the white mark on the leading edge of the hindwing.
Flights: (Uncommon) One from early April through early October.
Host Plants: Oaks and possibly Basswood.

Red-banded Hairstreak *Calycopis cecrops*

Identification: Underside with red band bordered with white on one side.
Flights: (Common) Two broods, early April to early October.
Host Plants: Sumacs and oaks.

Grey Hairstreak   *Strymon melinus*

Identification: Forewing gray with white band edged with black. Hindwing gray with orange patch near tail on both upper and lower sides.
Flights: (Common) Early April through October in 3 overlapping broods.
Host Plants: Clovers, lespedeza and mallows.

Eastern Tailed-Blue   *Everes comyntas*

Identification: Hindwing has orange spot at base near the tail. Males are blue above and females are dark above.
Flights: (Common) 4-5 broods starting in late March and ending in early October.
Host Plants: Clovers, bush-clovers and vetch.

Spring Azure   *Celastrina ladon*

Identification: Males are blue and females are violet-blue with black border. The underside has a fuzzy brownish-white background with dark spots. Spring Azures may be a complex of several species.
Flights: (Common) One brood in late March to late May.
Host Plants: Dogwood and viburnums.

Summer Azure   *Celastrina neglecta*

Identification: Male are blue and females are violet-blue with black border. Underside is silvery-white with distinct dark spots.
Flights: (Common) Probably 3 broods starting in late March and ending in early October. (Start before Spring Azures).
Host Plants: Smooth Sumac and Wingstem.

Northern Metalmark   *Calephelis borealis*

Identification: Two-toned brownish-red with indistinct marks, wavy lines and dark band. Females and males are similar. Underside is orange with dark brown spots.
Flights: (Uncommon) One brood, late June to mid-July.
Host Plants: Oblong-leaved Ragwort.

American Snout   *Libytheana carinenta*

Identification: Note the long palps and hooked forewing. This butterfly migrates regularly from southern states to our area but is unable to survive our winters.
Flights: (Uncommon) Irregularly migrates from south from May through October.
Host Plants: Hackberry.

Silvery Checkerspot   *Chlosyne nycteis*

Identification: A small butterfly but slightly larger than the similar Pearl Crescent. Note that the hindwing black spots have one or two with yellow centers.
Flights: (Uncommon) Two broods from late April to late September..
Host Plants: Asters, sunflowers and Wingstem.

Pearl Crescent   **Phyciodes tharos**

Identification: Submarginal band of black spots on the hindwing are without yellow centers. Crescents are usually visible below the spots. This butterfly is quite variable between broods.
Flights: (Abundant) 3 overlapping flights starting in April, ending in early November.
Host Plants: Asters.

Variegated Fritillary *Euptoieta claudia*

Identification: Orange with black bands and spots. Note the black doughnut-shaped spot near the leading edge of the forewing. The underside has no white spots - but the doughnut-shaped spot is visible.

Flights: (Common) 3-4 broods from April to early November.

Host Plants: Passionflowers and violets.

Great Spangled Fritillary *Speyeria cybele*

Identification: This is our largest fritillary with a brown basal area - darker in females. On the underside there is a light tan band between two rows of white spots that is much wider than the similar Aphrodite.

Flights: (Common) One extended brood Mid-May to late September.

Host Plants: Violets, particularly Common Blue Violet.

Aphrodite Fritillary   *Speyeria aphrodite*

Identification: Slightly smaller than the Great Spangled and the basal area is usually not as dark. The tan submarginal band on the underside hindwing is very narrow between the white spots.
Flights: (Uncommon) One extended brood from June to September.
Host Plants: Violets.
Big Meadows at Shenandoah NP is a good place to find them.

Meadow Fritillary   *Boloria bellona*

Identification: Somewhat similar to the Variegated Fritillary except that it is much smaller. Also note that the hindwings lack a black border. Most often seen nectaring low to the ground.
Flights: (Uncommon) 3 flights: April through September.
Host Plants: Violets.

American Lady　　　　　*Vanessa virginiensis*

Identification: Note white spot in upper forewing in the orange area and two large eyespots on the underside hindwing.
Flights: (Common) 3 broods from late April to early November.
Host Plants: Cudweed, pussytoes and Sweet Everlasting.

Painted Lady　　　　　*Vanessa cardui*

Identification: Note the lack of a white spot in the orange area of the upper forewing and band of small eyespots on the underside of the hindwing.
Flights: (Uncommon-Common) 2 broods in the south from April to October. Usually seen most in late summer most years.
Host Plants: Thistles, mallows, sunflowers and legumes.

Baltimore Checkerspot *Euphydryas phaeton*

Identification: (Uncommon) Our largest checkerspot with black wings with white and orange spots.
Flights: (Uncommon) One brood in mid-June.
Host Plants: Primarily White Turtlehead.
Several locations in Southern MD - the above was photographed at Big Meadows, Shenandoah National Park.

Mourning Cloak *Nymphalis antiopa*

Identification: Dark wings with yellow-white border.
Flights: (Uncommon) Mourning Cloaks may have only one brood per year. Butterflies that emerge in Mar-Apr go dormant through summer, emerging, Sep-Nov, to build up fat reserves for winter. Mating and egg-laying occur in spring.
Host Plants: Elms, hackberries and willows.

Question Mark   *Polygonia interrogationis*

Identification: Note the white "question mark" on the underside of the hindwing. If you study the upperside of the forewing of the Question Mark and the Eastern Comma, you will note that the Question Mark has a row of three black spots and a rectangular spot - the Comma does not have this spot. Note that there are two forms, the summer "black" form on the top row and the fall-winter "orange" form on the bottom row. The fall-winter form hibernates in leaves during the winter and lays eggs in the spring.

Flights: (Uncommon) April, June and early September are the best times to find them, but they can show up on most warm days.

Host Plants: Elms, hackberries and willows.

Eastern Comma   *Polygonia comma*

Identification: Note the thick white "comma" on the underside hindwing. Note the three forewing spots where the Question Mark has four.

Flights: (Uncommon) Like the question mark there is a summer form (May through August) and a fall form. The fall form can be seen in late summer and again in early spring. In the spring and fall, the forms can overlap.

Host Plants: Nettles, elms and hackberry.

Red Admiral *Venessa atalanta*

Identification: Red-orange band on forewing and border on hindwing. The underside lacks eyespots and is a mottled brown.
Flights: (Common) 2-3 broods from late April through October.
Host Plants: Nettles and False Nettle.

Common Buckeye *Junonia coenia*

Identification: Large eye spots on both wings. Underside varies with season - tan to reddish-brown in fall.
Flights: (Common) 3 broods from April through November.
Host Plants: Plantain and figworts.

Red-spotted Purple   *Limenitis arthemis*

Identification: At a distance can resemble a Pipevine Swallowtail which some think it evolved to mimic but it is slightly smaller and lacks tails. *This butterfly is also named Red-spotted Admiral.*
Flights: (Common) 2 broods, May through mid-October.
Host Plants: Unusually variable. "Black Cherry, willows, Serviceberry and dewberries.

Viceroy   *Limenitis archippus*

Identification: Slightly smaller than the Monarch but similar looking except for the dark submarginal band on the hindwing.
Flights: (Common) 3 broods from early May to mid-October.
Host Plants: Primarily willows.

Hackberry Emperor   *Asterocampa celtis*

Identification: There is a single eyespot on the forewing and a number of white spots. The underside usually has a grayish appearance.
Flights: (Uncommon) 2 broods, mid-May to mid-September.
Host Plants: Hackberries.

Tawny Emperor   *Asteroccampa clyton*

Identification: Larger than the Hackberry with tawny spots on the forewing - note lack of eyespot on the forewing. The hindwing has a row of dark spots, similar to the Hackberry.
Flights: (Uncommon) 2 broods, late June to late September.
Host Plants: Hackberries.

Northern Pearly-eye   *Enodia anthedon*

Identification: Medium sized butterfly. There are 4 or 5 eyespots on the forewings and 6 on the hindwings. The submarginal eyespots are surrounded by a continuous light colored line.
Flights: (Uncommon) 2 broods, late May to late September.
Host Plants: Grasses (Bottlebrush, panic, plume, Red Fescue).

Appalachian Brown   *Satyrodes appalachia*

Identification: 4 similar sized eyespots on the forewings and 3 submarginal darker brown bands on the underside - our other Satyrs have two.
Flights: (Common) 2 Broods, May through September.
Host Plants: Tussock/Upright Sedge and other sedges.

Carolina Satyr   *Hermeuptychia sosybuis*

Identification: Smaller than Little Wood-Satyr below but no large eyespots on the forewing. The upperside shows no eyespots.
Flights: (Rare) 3 broods, May through September.
Host Plants: Grasses (possibly Kentucky Bluegrass).

Little Wood-Satyr   *Megisto cymela*

Identification: The forewings show two large eyespots Note the fairly straight brown lines in contrast with the Carolina above.
Flights: (Common) 2 broods, mid-May to early August.
Host Plants: Grasses (possibly Orchard Grass).

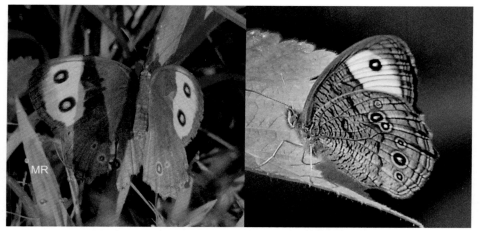

Common Wood-Nymph   *Cercyonis pegala*

Identification: Two prominent eyespots on the forewings surrounded by a yellow ("alope") or white patch ("nephele").
Flights: (Common) One extended brood mid-June through October.
Host Plants: Grasses (Purpletop, Poverty, Ky. Bluegrass).

Monarch   *Danaus plexippus*

Identification: Monarchs have elongated wingtips with yellowish spots. Males and females differ in that the males have a black scent patch and the females have thicker black veins. Monarchs lack the hindwing cross band that is seen in the Viceroy.
Flights: (Common) April through November.
Host Plants: Milkweeds.

Silver-spotted Skipper   *Epargyreus clarus*

Identification: Brown band on forewing that lacks the dark triangle of the Hoary Edge below. The hindwing has a white patch in the center not extending to the edge of the hindwing.
Flights: (Common) 3 broods, late April to mid-October.
Host Plants: Black Locust, tick-trefoils, Hog Peanut and Kudzu.

Hoary Edge   *Achalarus lyciades*

Identification: Note the dark triangle on the forewing and the white patch that extends to the edge of the hindwing.
Flights: (Uncommon) 1 or 2 broods from May to mid-July.
Host Plants: Tick-trefoils, Yellow Wild Indigo, lespedezas.

Long-tailed Skipper   *Urbanus proteus*

Identification: Long blue tails with blue at base of the wings.
Flights: (Rare) Wanders from the south, August to early October a few can show up in Northern Virginia.
Host Plants: Hog Peanut, tick-trefoils and Butterfly Pea.

Hayhurst's Scallopwing   *Staphylus hayhurstii*

Identification: Probably our smallest spreadwing skipper with a mottled appearance - note the scalloped wing edges.
Flights: (Uncommon) 2 broods, late April through mid-July.
Host Plants: Lamb's quarters.

Northern Cloudywing   *Thorybes pylades*

Identification: Brown with a few variable white spots on forewing. Unlike the Southern Cloudywing the face is dark brown.
Flights: (Common) One or two broods in May to August.
Host Plants: Tick-trefoils, bush-clovers and other legumes.

Southern Cloudywing   *Thorybes bathyllus*

Identification: Brown with a band of bold white marks that are mostly aligned. Note the white eyering and face (palps).
Flights: (Common) 2 broods from May through August.
Host Plants: Tick trefoils, bush clover, legumes.

Dreamy Duskywing — *Erynnis icelus*

Identification: The Dreamy and Sleepy Duskywings are very similar but note long palps and gray forewing band - Sleepy Duskywing has much shorter palps.
Flights: (Common) One brood mid-Apr to early May.
Host Plants: Willows and birches.

Sleepy Duskywing — *Erynnis brizo*

Identification: Similar to Dreamy but lacks the prominent gray forewing band and also note the short palps and chain-like band on the forewings.
Flights: (Uncommon) One brood in early May to late June.
Host Plants: Oaks, particularly Bear/Scrub Oak.

Juvenal's Duskywing   *Erynnis juvenalis*

Identification: Note the forewing spot and gray overscaling - in our area these features are diagnostic for Juvenal's. On the males, the white spots are not as prominent and the noted white spot may be faint.

Flights: (Common) One brood in early April through May.

Host Plants: Red and (particularly) white oaks.

Horace's Duskywing   *Erynnis horatius*

Identification: Horace's are similar to Juvenal's above but lack the gray overscaling on the forewings. They can be easily confused through May, but by June the Juvenal's should no longer be flying.

Flights: (Common) 3 broods starting in late April through September.

Host Plants: Red and (particularly) white oaks.

Wild Indigo Duskywing   *Erynnis baptisiae*

Identification: The forewing lacks the central white spot.
Flights: (Common) 3 broods starting in April through October.
Host Plants: Crown Vetch and Yellow Wild Indigo.

Common Checkered-Skipper   *Pyrgus communis*

Identification: Heavily checkered brown and white. Males have blueish hair-like scales around the inner wing and body.
Flights: (Common) 2-3 broods starting in April to early October - the first may be weak - usually common in late summer.
Host Plants: Velvetleaf, other mallows and hollyhocks.

Common Sootywing   *Pholisora catullus*

Identification: Small dark black butterfly with white spots on fore-wing and a few on the hindwing border. Note also the white spots on the head.
Flights: (Uncommon) 3 broods from May to August.
Host Plants: Primarily Lamb's Quarters.

Swarthy Skipper   *Nastra iherminier*

Identification: A small unremarkable skipper that is usually dark brown. Its lack of notable features is probably the best identification in our area.
Flights: (Common) 3 broods from May through September.
Host Plants: Little Bluestem (grass), possibly bluegrass.

Clouded Skipper   *Lerema accius*

Identification: Dark brown with one or two small irregularly shaped white spots in the center of the forewing. In females the spots are slightly more prominent. *Note underside view on Page 64.*
Flights: (Uncommon) 2 broods from May to mid-November.
Host Plants: Barnyard Grass and other grasses.

Peck's Skipper   *Polites peckius*

Identification: Hindwing has orange rectangles. Forewing has orange on leading edge and around black stigma on males. *See page 64 for underside view.*
Flights: (Common) 2 broods from May to early October.
Host Plants: Rice Cutgrass, Ky. Bluegrass, possibly others.

Fiery Skipper   *Hylephila phyleus*

Identification: Male is bright yellow-orange with dark brown spots. Note the jagged brown spots on the margins suggesting flames. The female has lance-like orange spots on the forewing. The underside is orange with dark brown spots - the spots tend to be more prominent in females.

Flights: (Common) 2 broods from June to late October.

Host Plants: Grasses (Crab, Bermuda and Redtop).

Indian Skipper   *Hesperia sassacus*

Identification: Male forewing is orange with a thin black stigma. Could be confused with the Fiery Skipper except the brown hindwing has square yellow spots that form a chevron and the flight dates do not overlap. Note also that the spots are concave outwardly.
Flights: (Uncommon) One in late May to late June
Host Plants: Little Bluestem, panic grasses and Red Fescue. Have been regularly found at Big Meadow, Shenandoah National Park.

Least Skipper   *Ancyloxypha numitor*

Identification: This is a very small skipper and flies weakly and
low to the ground in vegetation. The underside is bright orange with
slightly highlighted veins. The upperside is dark brown with some
orange around the margins.
Flights: (Common) 3 broods from April through October.
Host Plants: Bluegrass and Rice Cutgrass.

European Skipper   *Thymelicus lineola*

Identification: Slightly larger than the least skipper, it too has a
bright orange underside but the upperside is orange with black on
the wing margins that radiate thin black veins.
Flights: (Common) One flight in June.
Host Plants: Timothy, Orchard Grass, Velvet Grass.
Not common locally but common in mountain areas of VA and MD.

Little Glassywing   *Pompeius verna*

Identification: Note the rectangular white spot on the male and the square spot on the female. Differentiated from Crossline and Tawny-edge by lack of orange margin on leading edge of upper wing. Note white before antenna club. *See page 65 for underside view.*
Flights: (Common) 2 broods from late May through September.
Host Plants: Purpletop (grass).

Delaware Skipper   *Anatrytone logan*

Identification: An orange skipper with distinct dark veins. Note also the cell-end bar. Females are similar except usually show a thicker dark brown border on the wings.
Flights: (Uncommon) One brood mid-June to mid-August.
Host Plants: Bluestem grasses and Switchgrass.

Southern Broken-Dash   *Wallengrenia otho*

Identification: More orange than the Northern Broken-Dash. Male has "Dash" behind black stigma. Female is often indistinguishable from other female skippers. *See page 65 for underside view.*
Flights: (Uncommon) 2 broods from August to early September.
Host Plants: (Probably) panic grasses.

Northern Broken-Dash   *Wallengrenia egeremet*

Identification: Dull orange leading edge and two rectangular spots. Male has orange dash trailing from the black stigma. Female has two rectangular spots on forewing and a purple sheen (when fresh). *See page 65 for underside view.*
Flights: (Uncommon) 2 broods from early June to early August.
Host Plants: Deer Tongue, Switchgrass, other panic grasses.

56

Tawny-edged Skipper   *Polites themistocles*

Identification: The Tawny-edged and Crossline below, are very difficult to tell apart even from photos. Note the bright orange leading forewing edge of the male. The underside hindwing has a faint band of spots as does the Crossline below.
Flights: (Uncommon) 2 broods from May through September
Host Plants: Grasses (panic and bluegrass).

Crossline Skipper   *Polites origenes*

Identification: Males have conspicuous black (crossline) stigma on the forewing and tawny leading edge. Because of these skippers' variability in markings, it is very difficult to ID them, especially the females as they can look like several other species.
Flights: (Common) 2 broods from May to late September with gaps.
Host Plants: Purpletop and Little Bluestem.

Sachem

Atalopedes campestris

Identification: The male Sachem has a large black patch around the stigma - this usually makes the males easy to spot. The females have light colored chevrons with the same black patch that the males have. The males and females look different on the underside with the males showing a dark patch in the basal area and the females showing a series of lighter spots forming a chevron.

Flights: (Common) 3 broods from mid-April through mid-November.

Host Plants: Grasses (Bermuda, Crab and Goosegrass).

Hobomok Skipper   *Poanes hobomok*

Identification: Males are bright orange with a dark irregular brown border. The markings near the forewing apex are irregular. The females are similar but are darker brown and show more dark near the forewing base. Note the upper right female in a nearly white form which occurs occasionally. Also note the females muted chevron markings on the underside of the hindwing.

Flights: (Uncommon) One brood in mid-May to mid-June.

Host Plants: Panic grass, bluegrass, other grasses

Have been regularly found at Big Meadow, Shenandoah National Park.

Zabulon Skipper   *Poanes zabulon*

Identification: Males are orange bordered by brown. The leading edge is orange and there is a hook-like brown pattern near the apex. Note that there are no black veins in the orange patch of upper hindwing. The females are dark brown with light colored chevron markings. On the underside note the orange patch surrounded by brown on the males and note the white fringe on the females.

Flights: (Common) 2 broods: mid-April through mid-October.

Host Plants: Purpletop, Purple Lovegrass, other grasses.

Dion Skipper   *Euphyes dion*

Identification: Note the lighter-colored ray on the upper and underside hindwing. The male forewing is similar to the Crossline Skipper - it too has the hindwing ray.
Flights: (Rare) May through mid-September.
Host Plants: Tussock/Upright Sedge and Woodgrass.

Pepper and Salt Skipper   *Amblyscirtes hegon*

Identification: A dark brown and white skipper. Note the wing fringes that are checkered brown and white. Note the strong forewing spots.
Flights: (Rare) Late April through May.
Host Plants: Grasses (Ky. Bluegrass, Fowl Mannagrass and River Oats).

Dun Skipper   *Euphyes vestris*

Identification: A dark brown skipper that is mostly unmarked. Females usually show 2-3 small white spots. *See page 65 for underside view.*
Flights: (Common) 2 broods, mid-May through mid-October.
Host Plants: Sedges, possibly Tussock/Upright Sedge.

Ocola Skipper   *Panoquina ocola*

Identification: Distinctly elongated forewing. Note the two spots on the forewing and the darker outer quarter of the hindwing.
Flights: (Uncommon) 3 broods in the south. It regularly migrates north into our area mid-August to late October.
Host Plants: Rice Cutgrass.

Similar Butterflies

Pipevine Swallowtail

Black Swallowtail

Spicebush Swallowtail

Eastern Tiger Swallowtail

Tawny Emperor

Variegated Fritillary

Skipper Comparison

Hobomok

Hobomok

Zabulon

Zabulon

Sachem

Peck's

MR

Pepper & Salt

Clouded

KL

GM

64

Southern Broken-dash

Northern Broken-dash

KL

Dun

Little Glassywing

Fiery

Least

GM

Ocola

Indian

Similar Butterflies

Male butterflies collecting minerals

Relative sizes of butterflies

Index

Index

Index

88106337R00040

Made in the USA
Middletown, DE
07 September 2018